Look at Me I'm Learning Russian
(A STORY FOR AGES 3-6)

By Daniel Williamson

Illustrated by Kleverton Monteiro

Our fun phonetics help to explain how words are said in Russian. To write Russian we use Cyrillic, shown as the red letters on the left. Next to those are the Latin letters in black. The right column explains how each letter sounds.

Letter Pronunciation

а	a	'a' as in 'arch'		п	p	'p' as in 'pet'
б	b	'b' as in 'but'		р	r	rolled 'r'
в	v	'v' as in "vest"		с	s	's' as in 'set'
г	g	'g' as in 'goo'		т	t	't' as in 'toll'
д	d	'd' as in 'dad'		у	u	'u' as in 'put'
е	e/ye	'e' in 'year'		ф	f	'f' as in 'fifty'
ё	yo	'yo' as in 'yoga '		х	h	'h' as hook (aspirated)
ж	zh	's' as in Asia		ц	ts	'ts' as in 'lets'
з	z	'z' as in 'zoo'		ч	ch	'ch' as in 'church'
и	ee	'ee' as in 'bee'		ш	sh	'sh' as in 'sushi'
й	y	'y' as in 'yuck!'		щ	sch	'sch' as in 'cheese'
к	k	'k' as in 'kit'		ы	yi	between 'ee' and 'eh'
л	l	'l' as in 'let'		ь	'	make consonants sound softer
м	m	'm' as in 'met'		э	eh	'e' as in 'best'
н	n	'n' as in 'net'		ю	yu	'yu' as in 'yule'
о	o	'o' as in 'cost'		я	ya	'ya' as in 'yam'

First published in 2019 by Daniel Williamson
www.danielwilliamson.co.uk
This edition published in 2020
Text © Daniel Williamson 2019
Illustrations © Kleverton Monteiro 2019
Cover design © by Uzuri Designs 2019

Translation by Alexia Mankovskaya

All rights reserved. No part of this publication may be reproduced, stored in a retrieval system or transmitted, in any form or by any means, electronic, mechanical, photocopying, recording or otherwise, without the prior permission of the copyright holder.

ISBN 978-1-913583-01-9

www.danielwilliamson.co.uk

This book is dedicated
to my daughter
Carmela

I'm a small person in a big, big world!

Я маленький человек в большом-большом мире!

Ya ma-len'-kee-y che-la-vek v bal'-shom, bal' shom mee-re!

I know people bigger than me. Bigger people know more things because they start to learn when they are small.

Я знаю людей, которые больше меня. Большие люди знают больше, потому что они начали учиться, когда были маленькими.

Ya zna-yu lyu-dey, ka-to-riy-e bol'-she me -nya. Bal'-shee-e lyu-dee zna-yut bol'-sheh, pa-ta-mu shto a-nee na-cha-lee u-cheet-sa, kag-da biy-lee ma-lyen'-kee-mee.

Not everyone speaks English like me. Some bigger people speak Russian, some speak two languages!

Не все говорят по- английски, как я. Некоторые большие люди говорят по-русски, а некоторые говорят на двух языках!

Ne fse ga-va-ryat pa an-glees-kee, kak ya. Ne-ka-to-riy-e bal'-shee-e lyu-dee ga-va-ryat pa russ-kee, a ne-ka-to-riy-e ga-va-ryat na dvuh ya-ziy-kah.

I want to learn Russian too so I can speak to Russian speaking people and make even more friends!

Я хочу выучить русский язык, что бы разговаривать с теми, кто говорит по-русски, и завести ещё больше друзей!

Ya ha-chu viy-u-cheet' russ-keey, shto biy raz-ga-va-ree-vat' s te-mee, kto ga-va-reet pa-russ-kee, ee za-ves-tee es-cho bol'-she dru-zy-ey!

First I'm going to learn to count using the peas on my plate.

Сначала, я научусь считать, используя горошины на моей тарелке

Sna-cha-la, ya nau-chus' schee-tat', ees-pol'-zu-ya ga-ro-shee-niy na ma-ey ta-rel-ke

ONE
Один
A-deen

TWO
Два
Dva

THREE
Три
Tree

FOUR
Четыре
Che-tiy-re

FIVE
Пять
Pyat'

SIX
Шесть
Shest'

SEVEN
Семь
Sem'

EIGHT
Восемь
Vo-sem'

NINE
Девять
De-vyat'

TEN
Десять
De-syat'

Now I know how to count to ten! Look at me I'm learning Russian, learning Russian is Fun!

Теперь я знаю, как считать до десяти! Смотрите!
Я учу русский язык. Учить русския язык – это весело!

Te-per' ya zna-yu, kak schee-tat' da de-sya-tee! Sma-tree-te!
Ya uchu russ-kee-y ya-ziyk! U-cheet' russ-kee-y ya-ziyk – e-ta ve-se-la!

I wonder what to say if I meet a Russian speaking person? I think I would say - "Hello, how are you?" Then they would say - "I'm fine thanks and you?"

Интересно, что сказать, если я встречу человека, который говорит по-русски? Я думаю, надо сказать – «Привет, как дела?» и, наверное, я услышу в ответ «Спасибо, хорошо, а как твои дела?»

Een-te-res-na, shto ska-zat', es-lee ya fstre-chu che-la-ve-ka, ka-to-riy ga-va-reet pa-russ-kee? Ya du-ma-yu, na-da ska-zat' – "Pree-vet, kak de-la?" ee, na-ver-na-e, ya u-sliy-shu v at-vet "Spa-see-ba, ha-ra-sho, a kak tva-ee de-la?"

Then I would need to tell them my name. I would say – "Hello, my name is _____, what's your name?"

Ещё мне надо будет назвать своё имя. Я скажу «Привет, меня зовут _____, а как тебя зовут?»

Es-cho mne nada bu-det naz-vat' sva-yo ee-mya. Ya ska-zhu "Pree-vet, me-nya za-vut _____, a kak te-bya za-vut?"

Now I want to tell them my age and ask how old they are.
Let's see if I can remember the numbers!

А сейчас я скажу, сколько мне лет и спрошу,
сколько ей лет. Посмотрим, запомнил ли я цифры!

A se-chas ya ska-zhu, skol'-ka mne let ee spra-shu, skol'-ka yey let.
Pa-smot-reem, za-pom-neel lee ya tseef-riy!

Look at me I'm learning Russian!
Learning Russian is fun!

Смотрите! Я говорю по-русски!
Учить русский язык – это весело!

Sma-tree-te! Ya ga-va-ryu pa-russkee!
U-cheet' russ-keey ya-ziyk – e-ta ve-se-la!

I need to know how to say the things I like and the things I don't like, let's try some sentences!

Я хочу научиться говорить о том, что мне нравится и что не нравится. Давай попробуем!

Ya ha-chu nau-cheet-sa ga-va-reet' a tom, shto mne nra-veet-sa ee shto ne nra-veet-sa. Da-vay pa-pro-bu-em!

I like sunny days. I like to go to the park and play on the slide and swings!

Мне нравятся солнечные дни. Я люблю гулять в парке, кататься с горки и качаться на качелях!

Mne nra-vyat-sa sol-nech-niy-e dnee. Ya lyub-lyu gu-lyat' v par-ke, ka-tat-sa s gor-kee ee ka-chat-sa na ka-che-lyah!

I also love playing with my friends outside. Sometimes we play football, sometimes we play hide and seek!

Ещё я люблю играть с моими друзьями на улице.
Иногда мы играем в футбол, а иногда в прятки.

Yes-cho ya lyu-blyu ee-grat' s ma-ee-mee dru-z'ya-mee na u-lee-tse.
Ee-nag-da miy ee-gra-em v fut-bol, a ee-nag-da v pryat-kee.

I don't like when it's rainy and windy so I go to the cinema,
watch cartoons and eat popcorn.

Мне не нравится, когда идёт дождь и дует ветер.
Ну, тогда я иду в кино, смотрю мультфильмы и ем попкорн!

Mne ne nra-veet-sa, kag-da ee-dyot dozhd' ee du-et ve-ter.
Nu, tag-da ya ee-du v kee-no, smat-ryu mul't-feel'-miy ee em pop-korn.

My favourite thing to do is go for a picnic.
I like eating apple slices but I prefer bananas!

Больше всего мне нравятся пикники. Мне нравится есть яблоки, а бананы я люблю ещё больше!

Bol'-she vse-vo mne nra-vyat-sa peek-nee-kee. Mne nra-veet-sa est' yab-la-kee, a ba-na-niy ya lyub-lyu yes-cho bol'she

Last time I went to the park I saw a huge rainbow.
Let's see if I can remember all the colours!

Недавно, когда я был в парке, я видел огромную радугу.
Посмотрим, запомнил ли я названия цветов!

Ne-dav-na, kag-da ya biyl v par-ke, ya vee-del ag-rom-nu-yu ra-du-gu.
Pa-smot-reem, za-pom-neel lee ya naz-va-nee-ya tsve-tof!

RED	красный kras-niy
ORANGE	оранжевый a-ran-zhe-viy
YELLOW	жёлтый zhol-tiy
GREEN	зелёный ze-lyo-niy
BLUE	голубой ga-lu-boy
INDIGO	синий see-neey
VIOLET	фиолетовый fee-a-le-ta-viy

The colours of the rainbow are red, orange, yellow, green, blue, indigo and violet!

Цвета радуги, это красный, оранжевый , жёлтый, зелёный, голубой, синий и фиолетовый!

Tsve-ta ra-du-gee, e-ta kras-niy, a-ran-zhe-viy, zhol-tiy, ze-lyo-niy, ga-lu-boy, see-neey ee fee-a-le-ta-viy!

Look at me I'm learning Russian!
Learning Russian is fun!

Смотрите! Я говорю по-русски!
Учить русский язык – это весело!

Sma-tree-te! Ya ga-va-ryu pa-russ-kee!
U-cheet' russ-keey ya-ziyk – e-ta ve-se-la!

At home I have some different pets and they are different colours too! I have a brown dog, a black and white cat and a grey rabbit.

У меня дома живут разные домашние животные и они тоже разноцветные! У меня есть коричневая собака, чёрно-белый кот и серый кролик!

U me-nya do-ma zhiy-vut raz-niy-e da-mash-nee-e zhi-vot-niye ee a-nee to-zhe raz-nats-vet-niye! U me-nya yest' ka-reech-ne-va-ya sa-ba-ka, chyor-na-be-liy kot ee se-riy kro-leek.

My dog likes me to throw his ball for him, he always brings it back, it's his favourite game!

Моя собака любит, когда я бросаю ей мячик, она всегда приносит его обратно, это её любимая игра!

Ma-ya sa-ba-ka lyu-beet, kag-da ya bra-sa-yu yey mya-cheek, a-na fsyeg-da pree-no-seet ye-vo ab-rat-na, eta ye-yo lyu-bee-ma-ya ee-gra!

My cat likes to sleep on the sofa all day, he's a very lazy cat!

Мой кот любит весь день спать на диване, он очень ленивый!

Moy kot lyu-beet ves' den' spat' na dee-va-ne,
on ochen' le-nee-viy!

My rabbit lives in the garden, he eats carrots all day, they help him see better at night time!

Мой кролик живёт в саду, он весь день ест морковку, что бы лучше видеть ночью.

Moy kro-leek zhee-vyot v sa-du, on ves' den' est mar-kov-ku, shto biy luch-she vee-det' noch'yu.

At night time I get into my pyjamas, I love getting into bed for a story, then I close my eyes and slowly fall asleep, ready to learn more Russian tomorrow…

А я, когда темнеет, надеваю пижаму и ложусь спать. Я люблю когда мне на ночь читают сказки, а я закрываю глаза и засыпаю. Завтра я снова буду учить русский язык!

A ya, kag-da tem-ne-yet, na-de-va-yu pee-zha-mu ee la-zhus spat'. Ya lyub-lyu kag-da mne na noch' chee-ta-yut skaz-kee, a ya za-kriy-va-yu gla-za ee za-siy-pa-yu. Zav-tra ya sno-va bu-du u-cheet' russ-keey ya-ziyk!

This author has developed a bilingual book series designed to introduce children to a number of new languages from a very young age.

If you enjoyed reading this story, you will undoubtedly like popular rhyming picture books from this author which are also currently available.

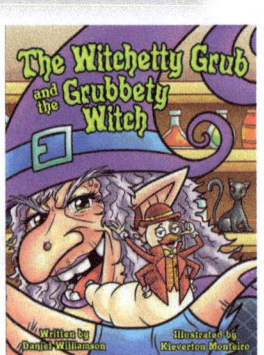
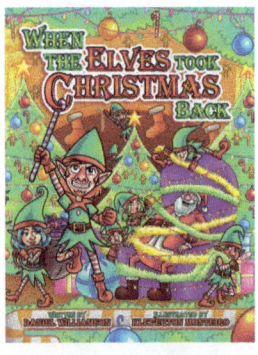

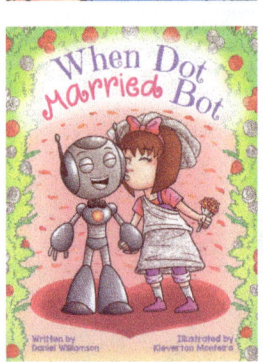

Message from the Author

I'd like to say a massive thank you to every single child and adult that read one of my books! My dream is to bring cultures together through fun illustrations, imagination and creativity via the power of books.

If you would like to join me on this journey, please visit my website danielwilliamson.co.uk where each email subscriber receives a free ebook to keep or we will happily send to a friend of your choice as a gift!

Nothing makes me happier than a review on the platform you purchased my book telling me where my readers are from! Also, please click on my links below and follow me to join my ever-growing online family! Remember there is no time like the present and the present is a gift!

Yours gratefully

Daniel Williamson

@DanWAuthor   @danwauthor   @DanWAuthor

www.ingramcontent.com/pod-product-compliance
Lightning Source LLC
Chambersburg PA
CBHW051251110526
44588CB00025B/2950